BY CRAIG [Gross]
with Rachel [...]

WHAT HAPPENS WHEN GIRLS
**GET REAL, GET HONEST,
GET ACCOUNTABLE**

YouthMinistry.com/TOGETHER

See-Through Life:
What Happens When Girls Get Real, Get Honest, Get Accountable
Copyright © 2014 Craig Gross and Rachel Ceballos

All rights reserved. No part of this book may be reproduced in any manner whatsoever without prior written permission from the publisher, except where noted in the text and in the case of brief quotations embodied in critical articles and reviews. For information, email inforights@ group.com, or go to group.com/permissions.

group.com
simplyyouthministry.com

Credits
Authors: Craig Gross and Rachel Ceballos
Executive Developer: Jason Ostrander
Chief Creative Officer: Joani Schultz
Editor: Rob Cunningham
Copy Editor: Stephanie Martin
Art Director: Veronica Preston
Production Artist: Brian Fuglestad
Project Manager: Stephanie Krajec

Scriptures taken from the Holy Bible, New International Version®, NIV®. Copyright © 1973, 1978, 1984, 2011 by Biblica, Inc.™ Used by permission of Zondervan. All rights reserved worldwide. www.zondervan.com The "NIV" and "New International Version" are trademarks registered in the United States Patent and Trademark Office by Biblica, Inc.™

ISBN 978-1-4707-1246-4

10 9 8 7 6 5 4 3 2 1   20 19 18 17 16 15 14

Printed in the United States of America.

TABLE OF CONTENTS

PART 1: FLIP THE SWITCH
(aka Being Open Is a Good Thing) 1

Chapter 1: Being Open Provides Safety. 11

Chapter 2: Being Open Leads to Depth 15

Chapter 3: Being Open Allows Freedom
and Liberty. 21

Chapter 4: Being Open Is Necessary. 25

PART 2: THE TO-DO LIST
(aka What Does It Take to Be Open?) 33

Chapter 5: It Takes Honesty. 35

Chapter 6: It Takes Courage 41

Chapter 7: It Takes Community 45

PART 3: RUBBER MEETS ROAD
(aka So How Do I Do It?). 53

Chapter 8: What Are You Looking For? 59

Chapter 9: What Does It Look Like? 71

Chapter 10: How Do We Keep This Going? 85

Conclusion: One Last Thing 87

PART 1:
FLIP THE SWITCH

(AKA, BEING OPEN IS
A GOOD THING)

Ladies, let us start by telling you this important truth: You're going to make it, and you have been made for a reason. If you're like most people, you struggle at times to be known for who you really are, to know the *you* who's hidden away because of shame you carry. From cutting, depression, bullying, and addictions, you might be dying to find meaning and value in your life.

We as a culture have lost the gift of community that God has given to all of us, so we all struggle with finding meaningful relationships. The Bible tells us to love God, but we can't forget we're also called to love our neighbor, to be people of deep, meaningful relationships because God knows this life is too hard to do alone.

We need accountability not for just accountability's sake; we need the openness to remind us that we will overcome and that these struggles are temporary. We've been called to be greater than our scars, to have a hope and a future. We as women have been made in God's image, and we need to live accordingly.

No man, no relationship, no amount of social media "likes" can take away the desire to be known. You need real people who love you for all your greatness and all your faults. It's time to get open and real and honest and even a little vulnerable. Some of the greatest things in life can seem a little scary, but we can tell you from experience that getting open is worth it.

The world you're growing up in looks pretty different from the one we did. When we were your age—which, honestly, wasn't all that long ago—it was possible to do something really stupid (and by "stupid" we mean, like, "over-the-top, beyond-your-dreams dumb") and not have it affect your future too much. Sure, your parents would probably find out about it, and you'd get in serious trouble at home. You'd probably get grounded for a time, lose your TV or Internet privileges, or have your car taken away from you, but rarely would you have to worry about some poor decision-making skills on your part destroying your entire world and making the global population hate you.

> In case you didn't know this already:
> Those days are gone.
>
> An even more sobering thought:
> They aren't coming back.

This is a different world now, and it seems to be changing ever more rapidly the longer we're around. Thanks to the Internet, along with humanity's collective ability to carry a powerful and technologically innovative computer/camera/communication device around in a pocket at all times, your world is under more scrutiny today than ever before. All the instant connectivity at your fingertips, combined with the ability to share just about anything on a whim through social media, means you have to be more careful about what you say and do than any generation before you.

These days, you just can't afford to do something dumb and have it plastered all over the Internet. Countless lives have been ruined, careers shipwrecked, trajectories altered, and futures abandoned because some teenager made a bad spur-of-the-moment choice and got in trouble either with the law or a social network.

In other words, the world you're living in is already open. Much more than any time before now.

>So you have to live smart.

>You have to embrace being open.

>You have to *live* open.

What do we mean by that phrase, that you should be "living open"? Well, we sure don't mean you need to reflexively blare everything you do, feel, see, and eat through every social media platform you have an account with. We don't mean you constantly point your phone's camera at yourself and post your every waking moment through a series of selfies, because selfies can take you only so far.

In fact, what we're talking about is the opposite of that. We're not opposed to you having a picture of yourself; we're just saying it's about time for you to be bringing another person or two into that picture.

We're talking about making yourself accountable.

We're talking about inviting one or two close friends into your world to help you live a strong life and achieve the many goals we hope you've set for your life—and so you can return the favor and do the same thing for them.

This is what we mean by living open. By being open. By embracing openness.

Now, before we can talk about being open, we have to make sure that what you hear when we say "be open" and what we mean are the same thing. Because right now, chances are good that they probably aren't. Maybe you, like a lot of people—if not most people—automatically think of something like "accountability" as a bad thing, like your parents holding you accountable by looking over your shoulder while you do homework or text your friends. This actually isn't the case! In fact, this isn't what we mean at all.

This might blow your mind, but it's true: Accountability is actually a *good* thing.

Let us repeat that, because it's important that you get it. And just to make sure you fully absorb this truth, we're going to put it on a line all by itself:

Accountability. Is. A. Good. Thing.

One more time, just to make sure, and we'll make it even simpler. Tweet-sized:

ACCOUNTABILITY = GOOD

Now it's your turn. Fill in the blank:

ACCOUNTABILITY = _____

The more I (Craig) have traveled and spoken about this idea of living an open life full of accountability, the more I've noticed that people automatically turn up their noses at just the idea of making themselves accountable to others. Mainly that's because when we hear phrases like "keep people accountable," they're inevitably tied to news stories about some CEO or investment banker or politician who did something illegal and who must now be brought to justice or made to pay for the innocent and unsuspecting lives they ruined.

With those images in mind, we tend to think of accountability as some form of punishment, instead of what it actually is: a life-giving boundary, a necessity in the modern world, a survivalist's backpack filled with a GPS unit, a box of Clif Bars and a packet of waterproof matches that will keep you alive in the wilderness that is life.

So the very first step you must take to becoming open is to flip the switch that resides in your brain. You must reframe this topic in your mind and start thinking about accountability in its true, positive light instead of the negative one that automatically springs to mind.

Being open isn't about restraining you or preventing you from doing something bad. It's about helping you do something good.

In fact, let's pause for a moment. Take a second to write down three things on the next page you think are good, and then write down a way that being open can be like each of those things.

3 THINGS THAT ARE GOOD

-
-
-

HOW IS BEING OPEN LIKE THOSE 3 THINGS?

OK, so it probably isn't enough for us to just tell you that accountability is a good thing; we're guessing you're interested in learning *how* it's good. We're glad you brought that up! With that in mind, let's take a brief look at four ways being open is a good thing. Those four things are:

- Being open provides safety.

- Being open leads to depth.

- Being open allows freedom and liberty.

- Being open is necessary.

Got 'em? Great. Now that we've taken an overview, let's look at each one a little more in depth.

By the way: For much of this book, Craig is the main voice speaking and sharing insights into accountability. So most of the time, when you see "I," it means Craig. Sometimes Rachel will jump into the conversation, especially in Part 3. We'll be sure to let you know when she's the one writing!

CHAPTER 1
BEING OPEN PROVIDES SAFETY

First off, let's define the kind of safety we're talking about here, because there are two different kinds. There's the smart, wise kind of safety—like buckling your seat belt when you get in the car or putting a protective case on your smartphone—and then there's the more reactionary, fear-based kind of safety—like never driving anywhere or having only a landline.

> I'm talking about the first kind.

To me, the concept of safety has nothing to do with curling up under the covers and refusing to interact with the world at large. Nor does it have anything to do with keeping your mouth shut at all times so you don't unintentionally say something that might possibly make someone mad (though this might be a good strategy at times).

When I'm talking about the kind of safety that accountability provides, I'm talking about the kind that sets you up with confidence so you can enjoy life to the fullest. This is the safety you feel just before you get strapped into a roller coaster: the comfort that helps you relax and enjoy the thrill of the ride because you know you're going to make it to the end all right.

We've all seen those movies or TV shows where a lost party of people is forced to wander through some mysterious wilderness or thick jungle, trying to find an ancient or magical artifact or trying to make it back to civilization. Inevitably, our heroes make their way through the dense foliage until they come across a rickety suspension bridge. You know the kind I'm talking about: the bridge made up of just a few ropes and some moldy wooden boards that somehow stretch across a scary-high drop (a drop that usually ends in a rushing river or pile of sharp rocks). Someone from the group will always test it out first, someone else in the traveling party will assure them it's safe, and then, when the person gets halfway across, a board will always break out from underneath their feet and fall down, down, down, taking forever to reach the bottom. Meanwhile, our hero looks on with wide eyes and held breath. Does the same fate await them?!?

Now, compare that kind of nerve-rattling, literally shaky experience from the world of fictional movies and TV shows to the types of bridges we actually experience in the regular world. From highway overpasses to interstate bridges to pedestrian footways in public parks, our world is full of bridges that we cross and *never think about*. That's how secure they are. That's how confident we are that these bridges will support us and carry us on our way without incident.

You may have heard about a 2013 incident from Washington state, when a semi truck carrying an oversized load of drilling equipment was traveling on Interstate 5, crossing the Skagit River on a bridge that had recently been inspected. Unfortunately, the truck driver accidentally made contact with the outside trusses that supported the bridge, causing a portion of it to collapse and plunge into the river below. Thankfully, no one was killed in the incident, though three people sustained injuries after falling into the river. The bridge was closed for about a month, disrupting the local economy and transit through that region.

The reason you may remember this incident is because it was news. Why was it news? Because bridge collapses in the United States—especially on well-traveled roads and interstate highways—are so incredibly rare. That's how much we've come to depend on them and how much confidence we have in them. We don't cross our fingers whenever we drive on an overpass. We don't even pause before crossing to check it out with a cautious toe. We just keep doing whatever we were doing.

The rickety suspension bridge that always gives way in the movies? That's a life without accountability.

The actual kind, the bridge with failures so rare that they're news? That's a picture of the safety that being open provides.

Accountability gives you unflinching safety and support, the kind of safety that lets you journey through life knowing that someone you love is backing you up, no matter what—and that you're doing the same thing for that person. No comfort compares to this kind of safety.

Now it's your turn. List five ways you can see accountability providing safety in your life:

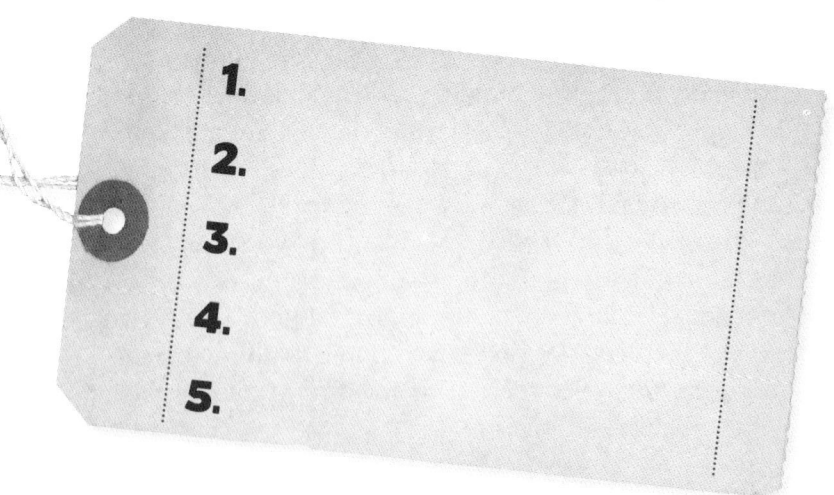

1.
2.
3.
4.
5.

14 BEING OPEN PROVIDES SAFETY

CHAPTER 2
BEING OPEN LEADS TO DEPTH

Have you ever been so into something—say, a book series, a TV show, some hilarious social media account, a sports team, a certain fashion brand, or whatever—that you had to go deep into it? You stayed up late several nights in a row inhaling the next volume in the trilogy or stuck in front of a screen thinking, *I should really go to bed, but…just one more episode.* Or maybe you've already planned out how you'll spend a large chunk of your next paycheck on a specific brand of shoes, or you're saving up for whatever product that tech company thinks up next.

The point is that most of us, if not all of us, like to go deep. In fact, I can't think of anyone in my world, even just among people who are my acquaintances, who is shallow and proud of it. Yes, we all have areas where we don't know a whole lot. In fact, most of our knowledge is of this type. There's a lot that we kind of know, a whole lot more that we don't know at all, and then a little bit that we know *a lot about*.

>That's depth.

Whatever interests you, that's what you go deep into. It's just a natural part of our human curiosity to want to know more—that's the way we grow and contribute to our culture and society.

But there's one thing all of us tend not to know very well, and some of us are actively opposed to going deep on that thing. What's that one thing?

>Ourselves.

Sometimes we're too scared to learn more about ourselves, and other times we just lack the resources to really dig deep into our own hearts and minds to discover who we *really* are and what *actually* makes us tick.

That's where accountability comes in. By putting accountability to work for you, by learning to be open with a select few people you invite into your world, you're able to focus on the task—sometimes difficult, sometimes pleasant—of deepening yourself.

One of the most deepening things about being open is the way you're able to draw each other out through the questions and conversations you'll inevitably have. This act of taking time and being intentional gives you the perfect opportunity to examine yourself and figure out who you *really* are underneath all the unnecessary stuff that life seems to pile on you.

You want to know a really cool thing about going deep? Once you're down there, you'll discover things you never even knew existed. It's like the deep sea, the part of the ocean that's so far down that sunlight can't get to it, making it completely dark. If you can go that deep, you'll uncover many different species of animals that boggle the mind, such as the cookiecutter shark, so named because instead of biting things and tearing them apart, it gouges out round plugs of flesh from its prey; or the lanternfish, a bioluminescent creature whose body glows in the dark; or the flashlight fish, so named because its eyes light up (organs underneath their eyes are actually filled with luminous bacteria, if you can believe it); or the anglerfish, that terrifying fish from *Finding Nemo* that's pretty much all teeth and has a lit-up ball hanging from its head. If you ever want some fuel for nightmare, just search the Internet for pictures of deep-sea fish and you'll find plenty.

The point, though, isn't to give you a lesson in marine biology. What I'm getting at is this: There are things about yourself that you're nowhere close to knowing yet. Some of those things can be fascinating, and more than a few of them are a little bit scary—almost as scary as that anglerfish. But regardless, if you're going to truly live the life God wants for you, then you'll eventually have to learn those things about yourself and learn how to live alongside them.

And that's where going deep can give you the boost you need. By going deep, you get to pull these things up to the surface and really turn them over, examine them, and learn about them—and by extension, learn about yourself. Pretty cool, huh?

You're in a stage of life right now that is, honestly, all about discovery, about navigating the space between childhood and adulthood and figuring out what to do with yourself in the meantime. You aren't a kid anymore, but you're also not a full-on, responsible adult yet. Going deep through accountability is a marvelous tool to help you through this.

Additionally, being open deepens your faith. How so? I give you Proverbs 27:17—*As iron sharpens iron, so one person sharpens another.* If you want to sharpen something, you won't get far by, say, waving it around in the air or dragging it along a gravel driveway. No, to sharpen iron, you have to use more iron. The interaction between the two might create a little bit of friction, but it will also result in a sharper edge.

In much the same way, by making yourself accountable in every aspect of your life, including your faith, you're stepping onto an elevator that will take you as deep as you want to go into your beliefs—and into yourself.

Now it's your turn. Write down five areas of your life where you want to go deep:

1.

2.

3.

4.

5.

CHAPTER 3
BEING OPEN ALLOWS FREEDOM AND LIBERTY

So many people look at accountability as being "sin management," a bunch of rules and regulations that define all the stuff you're doing wrong. You have your list of all the ways you can fail, and then you catalog those failures so you can puke them up during your accountability group meeting, feel ashamed, get barked at, and then leave feeling worse than before, knowing you're about to go back out into the world and return to not measuring up.

> Please don't do this.

> That's not what I'm talking about *at all*.

One problem with this approach is that it puts all the emphasis on your own efforts. *You* bear all the weight for all your slip-ups and mistakes, which isn't a support structure at all.

The other problem with taking the viewpoint that being open is basically like "sin management" is that it puts your vision entirely on what you're trying *not* to do, shifting you into a negative mentality and approach to your behavior. It's like flipping a visor down in front of your face (or Google Glass, if that makes it easier to picture—do an online search for Google Glass if you have no idea what I'm talking about) that fills your total field of vision with a giant, blinking sign that constantly screams at you: "DON'T DO IT!!!"

Instead of minimizing the things, thoughts, and behaviors in your world that you want to avoid, this approach essentially blows them up until they're the only things you can see. This makes them appear all the more inescapable and inevitable.

But there's good news here! When you approach accountability with the proper mindset—that it's good and beneficial—then being open frees you up to do the helpful things you want to do, to think the pure thoughts you want to think, to practice the positive behaviors you want to incorporate into your lifestyle.

That's the whole point of accountability, anyway—to feel free to achieve some goal or goals that make your life better. Think about it: Which would make your time at school better: focusing on the fact that you're getting an education that will serve you all your life or focusing on an intense desire not to fail each of your classes? Which point of view would send you running into school every morning with hope, and which one would send you trudging in with a sense of nearly unbearable dread?

When you're accountable, you pay attention to the positivity in your world and walk with freedom and liberty. Instead of looking over your shoulder worrying that you're about to get cuffed and arrested by the Sin Police, you can walk through life with your head held high and your eyes locked on the goals that lie on the horizon.

Starting to get a vision for the types of freedom and liberty you can have? Write them down here:

FREEDOMS & LIBERTIES

CHAPTER 4
BEING OPEN IS NECESSARY

Here's the thing about secrets: They almost always come out, and trying to keep them can drive us crazy. We instinctively know this, especially when we're contemplating doing something we know is wrong and start trying to convince ourselves it's really OK because "No ever needs to know about it."

Come on, you know you've told yourself this before. You can admit it. We're being open here.

The second we start thinking we can keep a secret is the second we have proof that being open is necessary.

Now, please understand that I'm not talking about harmless or helpful secrets. If you know a surprise birthday party is in the works for a friend, or if someone has confided something to you that they'd rather the whole world not know about, then you can hang on to those secrets. In the first case, it will come out eventually when your friend walks into a darkened room and everyone shouts, "Surprise!" In the other case, something you're told in confidence as a means of finding healing isn't so much a secret as private information not meant for public consumption. (I'm assuming, of course, you weren't told something that's illegal or that results in the person being hurt; if they're

25

in danger or doing something un lawful, you need to talk about it with an authority figure you trust.)

No, I'm talking about the types of secrets that lead to a downfall. Pro golfer Tiger Woods, former Congressman Anthony Weiner, Toronto Mayor Rob Ford—when their secrets came out, those guys went from being great at what they do to becoming a punch line.

The problem with secrets is that they grow larger and heavier until they eventually pull us under and become our undoing. That's why being open is so necessary—because when we're open, instead of keeping those secrets to ourselves, we can share them with one another, just as the Apostle Paul encourages us to do in Galatians 6:2—*Carry each other's burdens, and in this way you will fulfill the law of Christ.*

When we carry each other's baggage through accountability, we're spreading the weight around to many different hands and enabling each of us to walk upright and proud. Plus, if the second half of this verse is to be believed, then when we help each other this way, we're doing God's work. Plain and simple.

You know, I first started learning about being open when I was your age. Just after I'd completed my sophomore year in high school, my youth pastor at the time, a guy named Tom, asked me if I'd be interested in meeting with him one-on-one at a local McDonald's one morning each week. I wasn't sure if I could handle the early-morning time at first, but the more I thought about it, the more I realized how great it could be.

I've always been a pretty outgoing, confident guy. One reason I've been able to build a career as a speaker and minister is because of my natural abilities to connect with just about anyone. The only problem is that if you're this kind of person with those types of abilities, you can reach a place where you have a lot of acquaintances but not many deep friendships. I had a lot of the former and none of the latter. Tom offered me a lifeline when he reached out to me, so I took it.

In fact, as I pondered this even further, I began to see how good being open could be. I not only lacked a person or people in my life who I could go deep with, but I also lacked the capability to go deep. I didn't know how to do it, or even how to go about it. Tom was offering me the chance to have both: the skill set to go deep and the person to go deep with.

Tom and I started meeting, and it was great. I hadn't even known how beneficial being open would be for me until I started doing it. And once it began, I knew I would keep this a part of my life for as long as I drew breath on this earth. I finally had someone I could get real with: I could talk about my faith, my doubts and struggles, my fears about my past and my hopes for the future. I could talk about my temptations and the things I wrestled with on a regular basis. I could talk about anything and everything—and no matter what I said, it was OK.

So much safety. So much freedom. So much weight lifted off my shoulders, and all because I decided to take someone up on his offer to get open.

But here's the great thing, and the point I want to make: In addition to finding freedom and liberty in being able to unburden myself, I also had the wonderful opportunity to learn how to listen to someone else as they did that very same thing. That's because Tom took this opportunity to teach me about true openness and shared some of his own challenges. Now, he made sure that everything he mentioned was age-appropriate, and he didn't try to unload his adult responsibilities onto someone who was still a kid. I wasn't his sole accountability partner—I was just one of many high school students to whom he was teaching a valuable life skill. He opened up himself and showed me just a part of his inner world, and by doing so taught me how to listen and be trustworthy, how to care for something as valuable as another person's thoughts and feelings.

Tom and I met like this for about a year, until he suggested the following summer that we welcome my good friend Jake into our weekly meetings and go from being a sort of mentor relationship into something that more closely resembled an accountability group. I thought it sounded like a great idea, so I floated it to Jake. He agreed with me that it was something we could both use, so we started meeting regularly with Tom during our senior year in high school.

It was great. All the things in this book, all the practical advice and tools I give out when I talk about accountability—all that stuff got its start in those meetings with Tom, Jake, and me.

Tom taught us the overwhelming truth that accountability is good.

He taught us how we should go about keeping each other accountable.

He taught us the ins and outs of being open, being honest, and being real.

He taught us that the whole point of being open wasn't to sit across from someone and be their judge but to sit beside them and be their advocate.

He taught us that being open is all about talking and listening, both things working in concert to create a web of support that helps us carry one another's burdens.

Want to have a full and satisfying life now, through the rest of your school years, and well into adulthood? Then you need to get accountable.

You need to get open.

So what's it take to do that? Let's look a little more closely at the practical things you'll need to start living open.

YOUR TURN

Here are a few things that might prevent you from getting open. Circle the three you most respond to.

- Too vulnerable

- Too honest

- Fear of rejection

- Don't want to change

- Don't feel the need to change

- Happy with where you are

- Too busy

- Too hard

- Too much work

- No one to do it with

- I don't see my reason on this list; here it is:

  _____

Now look at the three things you've circled and write down the reasons they're lame excuses:

1.

2.

3.

PART 2:
THE TO-DO LIST

(AKA, WHAT DOES IT TAKE TO BE OPEN?)

OK, I hope that by now we've established that being open and staying that way is a good, healthy, honest, and positive thing for you. But now that you're convinced to try out accountability, you're probably starting to think up more than just a few questions about what to do next. Questions like:

- What sort of roads will I have to travel to get open?

- What sort of practical benefits will I see from traveling those roads?

- Are those two things somehow linked together?

Let's start by answering that first question, and once we figure it out, I think you'll have the answers to the other two.

Accountability has three basic components, three attributes it requires in order to work, and they aren't necessarily what you might expect. Those three things are honesty, courage, and community, and they work kind of like milestones on a road. If you don't embrace these three things, you'll just be spinning your wheels. Let's examine them more closely, and you'll see why.

CHAPTER 5
IT TAKES HONESTY

We've all been to the produce section of the grocery store, that magical, colorful place where everything is sold by the pound and you get to pick the amount you want. Maybe your mom sometimes asks you to run into the store and pick up a few things she forgot. Because most of us don't pick our own apples from a tree or grapes from a vine, it's kind of neat to select the items you want and put them on the scales in the produce section. That way you know how much you have and can figure out how much it'll cost to buy that plastic bag full of Granny Smith apples.

Then there's the deli, where you can ask the person behind the counter for a pound-and-a-half of roasted turkey, and they have a handy scale to measure it out. Except this time it's usually just a flat plate with a digital readout and a label maker. They'll measure out your pound-and-a-half of roasted turkey, push a button to spit out the label with a bar code and price, wrap up the meat, slap that label on there, and hand it over so you can go pay for it.

Scales have been a crucial component in the world of markets for a long time, though they haven't always been spring-loaded or digital. For centuries, the market scale was of the "balance" type. You probably know what I'm talking about: two saucers suspended by chains from a single beam that has a pivot in the center. Shopkeepers had a set of weights, so you'd order a pound of whatever you wanted, and they'd place their single-pound weight on one side. Then they'd measure out the thing you were buying on the other side until the scale balanced out. One pound on each side, right?

Except, not always. It became very common for merchants to shave down their weights by just a fraction so their single-pound weight became really, say, 15 ounces (in case you don't remember, there are 16 ounces in a pound). That enabled them to sell slightly less stuff for more money. Sure, they'd be cheating their customers, but they were willing to do that, especially because *everyone else* was doing it.

A couple of merchants in London knew this practice was going on—in fact, everyone knew it—and decided to be open and live honestly. They got together and started checking out each other's scales. One week one of them would verify the honesty of the other guy's scales, and then the following week they'd switch roles.

Word spread about these independently verified and trustworthy scales, so customers started taking their business to these merchants. When all the other merchants started losing business to the honest guys, they suddenly decided that honesty was the best policy. So they got in on the action, banding together with the original honest guys to form a trade association called (and this is real) the Most Worshipful Company of Livery Merchants.

This association started having a wider-reaching impact on even non-grocery merchants. Eventually they wound up influencing the British government to create an official department to oversee standardized measurements—a department that still exists today.

Kinda crazy how far a little honesty can go, isn't it?

The cool thing about honesty is that it really does cut through the nonsense like a bright ray of sunshine. Another cool thing about honesty is that it is, by definition, impossible to fake.

And if you try to fake your way through being open, you won't go far.

In fact, if you aren't prepared to be honest, then what's the point?

There's really no point in attempting accountability if you aren't also going to open yourself to honesty. To own up to the times when you don't behave like a shining star. To be vulnerable to a couple of people you can trust to hear your heart without judgment.

If you're going to hold back or misrepresent yourself in the context of accountability, then you probably shouldn't even mess with it.

But there's another side to this coin of honesty: You have to partner with other people who are committed to being open alongside you and who are willing to go completely down the road to honesty with you. You can't be the only vulnerable one, the only open one, the only honest one.

You must bring people into your picture of accountability who are *also* willing to take an unvarnished look in the mirror with you and accept whatever reflection shows up. That means both you and they are willing to not only ask honest questions but also to answer them honestly—and hear those answers honestly.

It can be tough to truly hear people at their most honest and vulnerable. Not only can it make us uncomfortable, but we sometimes don't know how to hear those honest answers *without being judgmental,* especially if a person we love has just admitted to some embarrassing or possibly reprehensible behavior.

Additionally, we also have to be ready to be challenged and disagreed with. We must be honest enough with ourselves to admit that we don't have all the answers, we don't have this world figured out yet, and we might *never* get that way. The last thing you need when you're trying to get open and stay that way is someone who tells you that everything you're doing is great and you don't need to change or improve anything. And you don't need to be that person, either.

But all these things require honesty. Are you ready to handle that? Because if not, then you might as well just be chatting about the weather.

Now it's your turn to "balance out the scale," just as the Most Worshipful Company of Livery Merchants did. Take a look at the spaces below; on one side write down an area of your life where you could use some honesty, and on the other side write down an honest response to that area.

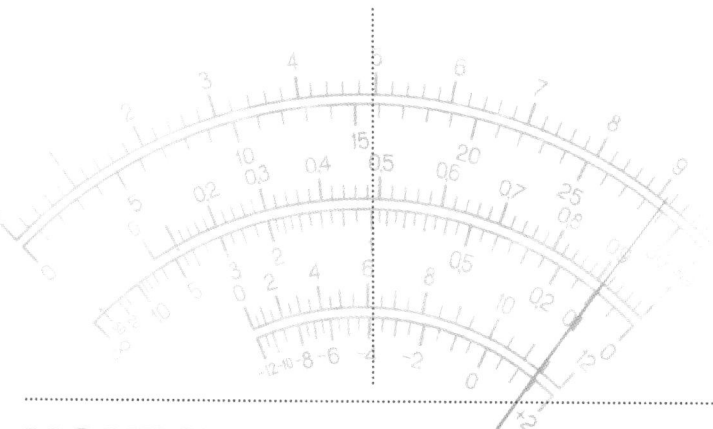

HONESTY NEEDED   **RESPONSE**

SEE-THROUGH LIFE

CHAPTER 6
IT TAKES COURAGE

Another crucial component of the accountability relationship, and one that goes hand in hand with honesty, is courage.

Think of honesty as the road map: You want to get from your house to this destination far away, and honesty is the map that will show you the way there. (Let's face it: No one uses maps anymore, so maybe we should call honesty the directions you got off the Internet or what came up when you typed an address into the Maps app on your smartphone.) But what good is a map if you don't have any way to travel? It isn't enough just to know your destination, or even to have the path to your destination outlined clearly. You must also find something to get you to that destination, because you won't get there with wishes and dreams.

So if honesty is the guide that provides the path that will show you how to get where you want to go, then courage is the vehicle that actually takes you there.

> In simple terms: Courage is honesty in action.

A few pages back, we talked about all the aspects of honesty that accountability requires. Well, all of them take courage.

Do you have to ask honest questions? You're going to need some courage.

Do you have to answer those honest questions, too? Guess what—that will take a little bit of courage as well. Actually, it will take *a whole lot of courage.*

Do you need to hear those answers with advocating honesty that simply listens without passing judgment? That can take some serious courage, too.

One thing about being open is that it provides us with an opportunity to deal with some of the stuff in our world or from our life that scares us—and courage helps us look into those scary places and tackle what we find there. Courage helps us deal with the tough stuff in our lives, from past hurts to current habits to future hang-ups. The accountability environment provides us with a safe place to deal with those things; courage provides us with the strength we need.

You'll notice that I'm talking about courage and fear in the same sentence, and perhaps that seems like a mistake to you. After all, if you have courage, doesn't that mean you're no longer afraid of something? Actually, it's quite the opposite! Courage is the boldness to admit you have fears yet are still willing to look them in the eye and face them down. Because the fact is, we all have fears. We all have scary stuff in our closets that we'd rather not talk about or deal with.

Honesty lets you admit those fears; courage gives you the club for smacking them in the face. Courage is the thing that lets you march confidently into battle, trusting that God will give you the strength to face your fears and that he'll be trustworthy in helping you conquer them. Especially because you know you aren't going to face them alone—you have your accountability partner(s) marching in there, right alongside you, ready to help you however they can.

That's what I mean when I talk about courage.

Now it's your turn. Think of the arrow below as a map; write your goals on the far end—that's your destination. In what areas of your life will you need to be courageous in order to reach that destination? Write those above the arrow.

GOALS →

CHAPTER 7
IT TAKES COMMUNITY

I have many friends, but a couple of my best friends are two guys named Ryan and Jake. They're the kind of people I'd go to the mat for in any situation, because I know they'd do the same for me. When I get in a jam and don't know what to do, these are the people (besides my wife) who I immediately think to call.

One thing I love about Ryan and Jake is how intense they are, how driven they are to make themselves better, both on their own and also when they get together. Ryan and Jake are both workout enthusiasts, if not necessarily healthy-living enthusiasts. These guys love to work out, to stretch their bodies to the breaking point, and they actually think grueling things like long bike rides and marathons are fun.

Anyway, Ryan and Jake were training for a triathlon (a two-and-a-half mile swim, followed by a 112-mile bike ride, followed by a little thing known as a marathon, which is running for 26.2 miles) and were really whipping themselves into shape. They don't live in the same city, so they were training with separate groups of people, athletes who could help them get better and better until they were in the kind of shape to perform in a triathlon and not die.

Amid this season of training, Ryan and Jake both had to come to a meeting in Southern California, where I live, so while they were together, they decided to go out one morning for a training run of 13 miles.

For fun.

These guys are my friends, but I don't always understand them.

Anyway, Ryan and Jake met up, stretched out, and did all the other stuff you have to do to prepare yourself mentally and physically for a 13-mile run. And just before they were about to start, they got into a conversation about the pace at which they'd run. For those of you non-runners, when you're covering a long distance like that, you try to keep a certain pace going, like a rhythm you can get into that helps you go the distance.

Jake, who was the strongest person in his training group back home, was confident he could maintain any pace Ryan wanted to run. Meanwhile Ryan, who intentionally trained with people who were stronger and faster than him, figured he could outpace Jake pretty easily. So between the two of them, they decided that Ryan could set the pace.

Then they were off. Ryan started off at a pace that would have them going about a mile every eight minutes, and Jake had no problem keeping up—for the first three miles or so.

By the fourth mile—not even a third of the way through their run—Jake began feeling the difficulty of the pace and started losing a couple of steps to Ryan. Now, instead of running side by side, Jake was just a few feet behind Ryan but still was managing to keep up. It was hard, but Jake did it—for the next four miles.

Around the eighth mile (if you do the math, you'll realize they'd been running for an hour nonstop at this point—I'm exhausted just typing that out), Ryan was still in his comfort zone while Jake was doing some serious work just to maintain forward motion.

So Ryan decided he'd kick it up to the next level and knocked about 30 seconds off the pace to make it a mile every seven-and-a-half minutes. Amazingly, though Jake lost another couple of steps and fell another few feet behind Ryan, he still managed to keep up. He was in complete agony, but he was there.

Three miles later, around mile 11 or so (roughly 90 minutes into their run), Ryan began feeling the burn of his natural limits, but he was determined to keep this quicker pace going, especially because Jake was still hanging on his heels. Plus, they had only two miles left, and Ryan wanted to finish strong.

But so did Jake. The last two miles were uphill, which made their desire to push themselves even greater. Neither runner wanted to let up, so although they were both getting winded by that point, they kept going and going and going. Running uphill is hard already; running uphill when all you've been doing for the last hour-and-a-half is running and all you want to do is beat the other guy but he won't slow down to let you—well, that's something else. That's Olympic-level dedication.

Both Ryan and Jake gutted out those last two miles until they finally got back to where they started, crossing the predetermined finish line in triumph. Jake fell to the ground in a very ungraceful manner, grateful to be done, while Ryan sort of crouched down and did his best to breathe and give himself a rest.

This story is a wonderful illustration of the power of community, the great things that can happen when we welcome others into our world and give them the go-ahead to challenge us in what we do. Neither Jake nor Ryan, running on his own, would ever have been able to keep up that pace. But because they were together, encouraging each other, spurring each other on through healthy competition toward a clear-cut goal, they found deeper reserves of strength and determination within them than they probably knew were there in the first place.

One thing we as people have seen time and again, both in the Bible and throughout history, is that it's extremely difficult to do anything worth doing by yourself. The Bible itself is packed with people who had help getting things done, even from the very beginning. God looked at Adam and said, basically, "This guy shouldn't be alone. I'll make someone to help him out."

Yes, a few people in the Bible accomplished some incredible feats solo, but you'll notice that those people generally didn't *continue* doing stuff on their own. David defeated Goliath by himself (well, God had *a little* something to do with it), but that's the only battle recorded in the Bible where David did his own thing. From then on, he had either an army or his "mighty men" to back him up.

Here's an interesting side note, as long as we're on the subject: David, by being off doing his own thing alone on the rooftop of his palace, put himself in a position to be tempted to sin with Bathsheba. (Check out the story in 2 Samuel 11.) It's because he was alone—instead of out with his army where he should've been—that he thought he could sleep with someone else's wife and get away with it. It's quite the understatement to say David could've used some accountability that day!

Scan through your history books, and you'll see person after person after person who had some help making

SEE-THROUGH LIFE   **49**

the world a better place. Why? Because life wasn't meant to be done solo. You need community to live a full life, and you need community to get open.

But community doesn't just fall out of the sky and hit you on the head. You won't wake up one morning and find community sitting on your front lawn with a hot mug of coffee. If you don't already have the types of friends and relationships in your world that you can transform into something for accountability, then you'll have to find them. (We'll discuss this in more depth in the next part of this book.)

The long and the short of it is this: We all need each other, and we need every part of the people we're being open with—the good parts, the bad parts, and everything in between. The truth is, we can do more together, go further together, climb higher together, go deeper together than we ever could trying to go solo.

Honesty, courage, and community. Those are the three things you absolutely must have in your world if you're going to get open.

YOUR TURN

Take a few moments to think about honesty, courage, and community. Which of these three things will be the easiest part of being open for you? Which will be the most difficult? Write down your reasons in the spaces below.

1.

2.

3.

PART 3:
RUBBER MEETS ROAD

(AKA, SO HOW DO I DO IT?)

Ladies, have you ever met someone who looks nothing like their social media profile photo? They have the classic selfie with every filter, makeup, contour, and perfect angle for the shot, but then you see them in real life and are blown away by how *different* they look.

We live in a world where we can reinvent ourselves with a simple photo, a perfect blog, or a creative tweet. The more open we seem to be as a culture, the more we can fear placing our "real" selves out there. But being really open means we open up ourselves to let people see the real us: the genuine, imperfect, cranky, sinful, bruised, and broken us. I (Rachel) believe in the old saying, "We're only as sick as our secrets." True freedom is found when we acknowledge all the ways we can't make it on our own and need help from God and others.

Now that we know accountability is a good thing, and we know what it takes, we can turn our attention to the practicality of it all. In other words, how do we get it?

One of the greatest gifts God has given us is the ability to have community with one another. We've been created to know people and to be deeply known in return, and although you might have 1,000 friends on Facebook and 500 followers on Instagram, it's really hard—logistically impossible, actually—to get deep with that many people.

That's why you need to make sure your accountability group is a manageable size and is really only a handful of amazing ladies. I always think if Jesus had no more than 12 disciples, then who are we to argue? Keep your group size small so you can be really intentional with each person in your little tribe. You need solid women who are dedicated to going down the road of life with you and who will expect the same of you in return.

What kind of women? You need women in your life who will tell you that cutting will never release the pain and that you are more than your scars.

You need women in your life who will tell you that throwing up every meal won't fix the way you see yourself in the mirror.

You need women in your life who will remind you that you were created in God's image and that when God said, "It is good," he was talking about you.

You need women in your life to tell you the truth about the men who surround you and whether the guy you're dating/liking/loving/crushing on is a man who deserves your attention or one you should run from.

You need women in your life who can hear your deepest, darkest secrets and still look you in the face and tell you that you are loved.

You need women in your life who encourage you to pursue your goals and dreams, who will be your biggest cheerleaders and will know that you're amazing.

You need women in your life who will tell you to stand up and find your voice and to never conform to the world's expectations of you.

But a danger of a safe community like an accountability group is that we can easily come every week to share and throw up word-vomit and then just leave. This makes you a consumer who never learns how to really listen to others and be fully present. Just sitting in a circle and thinking about tomorrow's outfit choice isn't really listening.

I assure you that you and your friends struggle with many of the same issues. Really listening to someone also isn't thinking about how to fix that person or preparing the perfect response. Great listeners are present in the moment and can sit with one another during good and bad times.

Learn how to really listen to others and give them your full attention. Instead of thinking of anything else, be there *right in that moment.*

This group will take courage for everyone involved. You need to be committed and agree to not only learn how to open yourself up for accountability but to learn how to be there for other people. The bravery comes when you realize that even though you may have been hurt in the past, being open within the safety of your group can bring incredible healing and wholeness.

And ladies, before we go any further, we have to talk about gossip. It's a sin committed by both guys and girls, but let's be honest: Women tend to struggle with gossip just a little more than the dudes do. With that in mind, here's a rule that should apply to every small group: *"Whatever is shared in-group, stays in-group. Seriously, anything."* Sometimes it even helps to make each girl sign a covenant or contract in your group that contains rules.

Here are three house rules I (Rachel) have used in the past.

- First rule: This group is a place of safety, and what you say here stays here. If this rule is broken, you risk being asked to leave.

- Second rule: Show up faithfully every week, because that's one of the greatest ways to show respect to everyone else.

- Third and final rule: We always end the night with prayer, believing that God is our strength and salvation, and that nothing is impossible with God.

These three rules let everyone know from the very beginning of your group that you all have the truest sense of safety when it comes to sharing. Everyone needs to know that what is shared each week won't be spread to friends/husbands/boyfriends/neighbors/moms.

Gossip always reveals the darkest part of our soul—the part where we try to hide our own insecurities by either putting others down or making ourselves feel bigger for the moment. I know gossip is a hard thing to kick, but we must rise above gossiping for the sake of our own insecurities. Just imagine what could happen if, instead of gossiping, we focused on speaking greatness about the women around us and pointed out all the areas where God is visible in their lives. We would become women who bring life with our words rather than hate and spite that only break others down.

Sound good? Great! Let's look at the simple ways you can get and maintain accountability. Every girl can say she wants to get open and be held accountable; the difficulty lies in making your accountability effective over the long run.

CHAPTER 8
WHAT ARE YOU LOOKING FOR?

We all have the desire to be known and experience deep and meaningful relationships that go past the surface. I (Rachel) am sure you're wondering, *"Where can I find these amazing women,"* or *"How do I actually get and maintain an accountability group?"*

I believe God wants us to have accountability as a priority in our lives. I'm currently in an amazing accountability group with women who are all searching for the same things I am. When you pray and ask God to open your eyes to see what is around, don't be surprised if you find women close to you who need a group like this just as much as you do. In fact, I love that it might force you to be bold and talk deeply with people around you! And this is the kind of woman that God created you to be: to speak truth, love, and care into the relationships God has placed around you.

Here are some basic guidelines of what to look and pray for:

GENDER

When it comes to real accountability, you need to be in a group with only other women. I (Rachel) know that if dudes are in the room, I can't get really honest about the things I struggle with as a woman. And most guys have no clue what it's like to be a woman and all the crazy, unique things that make us female (just talk about your period, and every guy brain just shuts down).

Women can understand the struggle to be a God-honoring woman in the world today, and issues such as cutting and body image are a reminder of how young women are dealing with their pain. Women understand that sometimes we're our worst enemies. It's a long process to begin walking with God and learning to see yourself through his eyes, and you need women who understand these unique battles.

AGE

You also need women somewhat close to your age. Although it's essential to have older women who are further down the road of life to mentor you and show you that you can follow God throughout your life and survive anything, accountability partners need to be around your own age because your struggles aren't just your own. When people really become open with each other, they find freedom in the knowledge that we aren't so different. The sins and struggles that weigh you down are usually the same burdens your friends are struggle with, too. Find girls your own age, and as you find freedom in your own life, it will be a guiding light to those around you who are in the same place.

Take a minute to list some girls who you might consider welcoming into accountability with you. List as few or as many as you'd like:

ACCOUNTABILITY

BACKGROUND

What's your background like? Do you love to sing? Do you dance? Are you an artist? an athlete? Do you love to read? Do you come from a large family or a small one? Have you grown up in a Christian family, or are you the first follower of Jesus in your family? Would you say you've had a pretty crazy past, or have you always followed the rules?

These are just a few of the life events and personal passions you possess that make up your background. No other girls have the exact same background as you, but if you look around, lots of girls share many of those similarities. Life is better when you have friends who can teach you new things to learn and enjoy, but when it's time to get deep, you need to understand one another.

Girls who have a similar background as yours are the kinds of people you want to be in accountability with. Why? Because you need people who will understand your struggles and who have maybe even experienced some of the same things. Some people will never understand you, and for accountability it's all about getting real and honest. You need a variety of women who have a similar life story!

List some girls who have a background similar to yours:

SIMILAR BACKGROUND

POINT OF VIEW

By your point of view, I'm talking about the way you see the world. This includes your opinions and preferences, from politics to theology to favorite sports, teams, music, and movies. That kind of stuff.

So when you're looking for someone to get accountable with, you'll want to find someone with a similar point of view to yours. Notice I didn't say the *exact* same point of view, but *similar*. There's a reason for that.

The way we grow as people is to have our ideas and preconceived notions challenged by outside viewpoints. So although it's good to have someone in your corner who can understand where you're coming from and who can champion you in what you believe and think, you also want someone who will push you to grow in ways you wouldn't ordinarily expect.

By forming an accountability relationship with a person or people with a point of view that's similar to yours, you're finding common ground where you can relate. At the same time, you're leaving the door open for growth in both directions—you can grow from their input, and they can grow from yours, which is really the point of being open, isn't it?

On the next page, list some girls who have similar—but not the exact same—point of view that you do:

SIMILAR POINT OF VIEW

TRUST

One of the first accountability groups I (Rachel) ever joined had a girl I just couldn't trust. I felt like everything I said in-group was going to be a conversation between her and random people later that night. I'd sit in our group and look at her face and think, *I'd rather tell all my secrets to a random Taco Bell employee than to her.* My gut instinct was that she was untrustworthy, and my gut instinct was right—sadly, she later was booted from the group because she couldn't keep secrets.

You need people whom you can trust and who can trust you. There's no need to keep girls in your group who thrive on drama. Set the rules from the beginning, and if someone in the group breaks trust, then confront her personally. Don't create more drama by avoiding the hard conversations or becoming a gossip yourself. By being honest in a loving way, you're becoming a healthier person.

Really loving someone else means helping her stop destructive habits and break addictions to drama. This also creates a bond that allows you to grow deeper in your relationships and to trust one another to actually get open. The ladies of your group become your "ride or die" chicks. They always have your back and take your secrets to the grave, and that's a beautiful thing.

List some girls you know you can trust. If there are any girls who you might have a doubt about, or maybe they're known for their gossip, then they might not belong on your list. You want girls whom you can fully trust and will be your small tribe:

TRUST

STAGE OF LIFE

Are you a student, full-time worker, no-time worker, or maybe just trying to figure out what to do with your life? You need to be in a group with other women who are in similar stages of life.

When you've passed through one life stage and into the next, it's easy to forget all the goals, dreams, drama, and pain of the past, so you need people who are walking the same road of life as you because they can help spur you on to do what you need to get done. If you're in high school and need to get off the couch and finish your college applications, then your fellow ladies can encourage you to finish them—and also provide good advice about what they did themselves.

Relationally, you need to be in the same stage of life so that when it comes time to talk about dating, dealing with parents, and even handling stress, you're all speaking on the same level. It's good to have people in your group who have different interests and goals, but you need to be in the same stage of life to really connect.

On the next page, list some girls who are in the same stage of life as you:

STAGE OF LIFE

So those are the similarities you want to have: *gender, background, point of view, trustworthiness*, and *stage of life*.

Now look at your lists for all those criteria and see how many times you listed the same person. I'm guessing you've written down at least one name in all five lists. If so, that's someone you can get accountable with.

But what if you don't have a clear person after making your lists? That's why you prayed! You can still use the lists you just made to narrow down potential candidates, trusting that God will guide you to the right accountability partner(s).

In either case, whittle down the possibilities until you have two to four people, and then approach them girl-to-girl (preferably when you're by yourselves) and see if they're interested and willing to be open.

CHAPTER 9
WHAT DOES IT LOOK LIKE?

Now that you have one or two people (or three at the most) to join with you on this adventure to openness, let's get super practical and talk about what your accountability meeting might actually look like. What sort of routine should you have? Where should you meet? What should you *do* when you meet? And how can you set this thing up to have a bit of longevity?

Let's take a look.

ROUTINE

Whether your group meets every week or every other week, you need to set a schedule. We live in a world where the pace is frantic and hectic, and sadly it's just the way we like it. The busier we are, the more we seem to be too busy to get honest and open, but forming accountability and true community with one another takes time and nurturing. We have to learn to slow down and stop using busyness to cover up some of the deep issues we're facing.

Plan a schedule with your group and stick to it. Consider that time of being with your girls as a gift, and don't schedule other things during it. After all, we know that where you put your time is where you put your heart.

Below is a typical calendar week, from Sunday to Saturday. Write in some possible times when your group can meet.

SUNDAY

MONDAY

TUESDAY

WEDNESDAY

THURSDAY

FRIDAY

SATURDAY

WHAT DOES IT LOOK LIKE?

SETTING

Location, location, location. Have you ever tried to tell a deep, personal secret inside a Starbucks? Probably not! You can't because everyone, including your third-grade teacher, is there getting a triple-whip Frappuccino. You need a safe place where you'll be able to really be open. While I (Rachel) love to meet my friends in coffee shops and other places, I almost always have the serious conversations in my home.

Accountability is all about being able to share and be transparent. So you'll need a place that's cozy and inviting, whether you find someone who has a room in their house for you to meet each week or connect at a different house each week, like my group does.

It's all about what's available and what works. Trusting one another means you feel safe, and the right location provides a space that allows you to be open and trusting in the first place.

One of my favorite things is to make our meeting place feel like home. I like to have tons of coffee and a few snacks available, and then I light some candles. Spending the time to create space for other people makes a difference when it comes to feeling safe and open. If hospitality isn't your gift, someone else in your group will most likely love it. And if no one has the hospitality bone in their body, find someone who does and see if she'll host your group. So much community can happen when people share the table together, and deep connections can be made over simple meals. Breaking bread and making a sacred place where girls can come together each week is an art.

If meeting at a physical location isn't possible, then you can turn to technology as an option. This works really well for Craig's group, which meets through a free conference-call system. But you can also use video conferencing programs that are generally available for free on most computers, such as Skype or, for you Apple users, iChat AV. Google Plus currently has video "hangouts" that can work really well, too, but you'll need a Google Plus account for that.

Ultimately, it doesn't matter *where* you meet—just make sure you're meeting regularly and taking full advantage of the time you have together.

Take a few moments on the next page to list all the incredible places you might be able to meet, or even list the people who might be able to host you in their home:

MEETING PLACES

FORMAT

So you have a fantastic location and possibly a delicious meal. You know the days you meet, and you have your tribe of fellow girlfriends. What now? Do you just tell all your deepest darkest secrets, pray, and then leave?

Sorry, word-vomit isn't what we're looking for. Here are a few ideas that have worked for me (Rachel) in the past, but don't let it stop here:

- *Always begin with prayer and ask God to bless your time together.* It's amazing what happens when a group of women come together and ask God to reveal all the areas where we bring life or death. We're able to ask God if our life has shared his light or if our actions have brought darkness into the world.

- *Start with this week's "highs and lows," which are exactly what they sound like.* The highs are the moments that brought you great joy and great connection with God, things to celebrate and be thankful for. The lows are those things that have knocked you down this week and need to be brought out into the open. This isn't super in-depth but instead helps you share more about the week's joys and struggles and begin your time together.

- *Ask the regular general questions.* (See the list that begins on the next page.) These questions are a great way to start each week's meeting.

- *Ask the specific questions.* We'll talk more about this in a moment, but these questions are more specific to each person.

- *End with a closing prayer.* This is one of the main agreements you've made in your accountability group. It helps you recognize that you aren't the ones who have to save each other. It's by God's strength and grace alone that we go forward, so end the group with the peace that God is in control. I also love to take this time to write down each person's prayer requests, so when I open my phone or journal or even scrap of paper, I'm reminded to pray for my girls.

- *Discuss things further, if you decide to.* It's always good to have a final moment with your girls before you head out into the world. Take this time to make sure any final thoughts, questions, or concerns are voiced. Share your gratefulness for each woman in your group, and thank them for being so honest and transparent.

- *Dismiss.* Head home! Don't sabotage an amazing group time by then staying an extra five hours after all is said and done. I've been guilty of overstaying my welcome if I get caught in great conversation. Always be respectful of other people's time and maybe their need to have you out of their house. I like to say, "You don't have to go home, but you can't stay here!" In the most loving way, of course.

ASK

In an accountability group of women, it's crucial for each person to know that she has a voice and to share equally. Make sure no one in the group hogs all the time. Some girls can talk forever and may even hijack each group time; you have to find a loving way to ask Miss Chatty McGee to tone it down. Make it clear from the beginning that each group meeting should be a place where each girl is expected to share and each person is aware of how long she's sharing.

Here are some ideas for questions you can ask in your group. Look at the following list and select a few that you think would be good for your group. Or have each member of your group pick one or two questions that she thinks should be asked of everyone, making the process all the more democratic. Here are the questions:

- How was your week?

- Did the things you said and did this week make your life better? Did they represent you well to the rest of the world?

- How have you treated people who are important to you this week? Did you honor them and treat them with grace and generosity?

- Did you use any of your words as weapons this week, either to someone's face or behind their backs?

- What about anger? Are you angry or resentful toward someone? Are you holding on to that anger or letting it go?

- What about your stuff? Have you been trustworthy with your money and belongings this week?

- Have you indulged in lusts or anything of a sexual nature (porn, masturbation, sexting, sex of any kind), whether physically or mentally?

- Have you caved in to any of your addictions or weaknesses this week?

- Were you bad to your body this week by overeating, undereating, cutting, using body-hate language, or anything that doesn't treat your body as the image of God he created it to be?

- Did you use your sexuality in a way that wouldn't please God?

- Did you use your sexuality for attention this week?

- Did you feel the constant need of approval from other people?

- Did you carry bitterness toward anyone?

- Did you struggle with jealousy of any kind and toward anyone?

- Have you talked badly about anyone behind his or her back or allowed gossip to be a part of your week?

- Were you honest and truthful in all you did?

- In one or two words, state how you're feeling emotionally right now.

- If you were triggered and this trigger was new, how can you avoid it in the future?

- State one lie you've told someone in the past week, or a secret you're keeping from someone else or this group.

- Did you lie to me/us in your answers to any of these questions?

When you look at these questions, you can see they're great kick-starters for you and the girls to start with, but we all know the issues we struggle with a bit more. Add your own questions as time goes by and as you begin to know the specific needs and struggles of your group.

What do I (Rachel) mean? Well, let me give you an example from my own life. I know that when I meet with my girls, we begin by asking ourselves all the dreams and hopes we have for our future, and we discuss all the things that just seem to get in the way.

Personally, I've always struggled with issues that seem to come from being a people-pleaser and putting others' opinions about me above my own. I know the sin of people-pleasing was bred in me from an early age. What's so difficult to break about this sin is that most people don't even know they struggle with it. So many women I meet spend a crazy amount of time worrying what other people think of them—they don't live in the present moment.

The crippling sin of people-pleasing is so common among young women that we don't address it. But the beauty of our small group is that I've taken the time to make my struggles known to our group, and each girl has the ability to call me on my struggles. Usually the other girls can see if I've let worry and fear creep into my life and cause me to stumble. Fear and worry are two areas that will usually point you toward an issue that needs to be addressed.

This question has always helped me point out some of my darkest issues: "Where in your life does something seem to overwhelm you and cause you to lose trust in God?" The girls in my group are able to zero in on the areas of my life where fear has taken over and can gently remind me that that isn't how God has created me. Sometimes they text me encouragement throughout the week, or other girls meet one-on-one with me to talk more in-depth and pray with me about issues that have seemed overwhelming.

At times, we as a group have asked other girls to think about possibly seeing a professional counselor or therapist. Issues of addiction, self-abuse, body hatred, depression, and past abuse are all too common for women. Every group of girls needs to know when its members should encourage individuals to see a professional. Your role in the group might be to give the support they need to speak up and get help. So many girls don't get the help they need because they feel so alone. Your job isn't to fix other girls but to be someone who won't let them stay in a place of dysfunction.

One of the greatest things about living a life of accountability is that we aren't just saying we want to grow in our faith; we're *actively pursuing* a life after God. The other women in my group are there to point me back to God's truths in my life when I seem to stumble and forget. The longer you live a life of accountability, the more goals you're able to set and actually meet, because over time you can see the destructive habits in your life and create ways to avoid or stop them altogether.

Now is the time to come up with your specific question or questions. What do you want your group asking you from week to week? Get honest and write down the questions you seem to ask yourself all the time. This is the question (or questions) you need your girls to ask you personally each week. Write them down:

MEETING QUESTIONS

CHAPTER 10
HOW DO WE KEEP THIS GOING?

God has given you a fantastic group of women, so it's important for you to take the time to nurture those relationships. Find the common things you all love to do, and then go out and do them! Sometimes you need to be reminded that you've been placed in this group for a reason.

Some of my (Rachel here) greatest lifelong friendships have come from the women in my accountability group. We take turns meeting at one another's house or apartment and have a rotation for making dinner for one another. I look forward to our meetings because not only do we encourage one another but we're also a family. Prayer, honesty, laughter, and tears have bonded us. Find the things you can do together as a group that remind you you're more than a task list or another thing to check off the list. I love that we make dinner each week because sometimes the simple act of feeding one another shows love on a deeper level. Something happens when people sit around a dinner table and make time to be present.

I've also been part of groups that go and serve together. We focused on helping one another achieve our goals, but we also served others. Go the extra mile together and get outside your comfort zone. Serving the underprivileged in your area or finding service projects to do outside your group connects you even more deeply to one another. Throughout the week, email, text, or call the girls in your group, and find different ways to bless each other. Bake something, write a card, go visit a girl at work or school, or buy her a puppy (get her family's permission first!).

Every girl has been blessed with gifts that can bless others. Learn what it means to serve other people, and you'll be blown away by how you receive blessings in return.

CONCLUSION
ONE LAST THING

Take the time right now to figure out what's been holding you back from really finding a group of people to get honest with. You can't get open with someone if you've never found out what issues are holding you down. You deserve to find freedom from fear. God has incredible plans for your life. Be brave and find a group of women, because it's never too early to get open, and you're never too young to be accountable.

If you've done all the exercises in this book, you're now not only fully convinced you need accountability, but you've also done all the practical work on the front end that being open requires. Fill in the blanks on the following pages, then copy this list and post it where you'll see it regularly as a reminder that you're on the path to being open.

My Goals

My Accountability Partner(s)

Meetings

Day:

Time:

Our Meeting Location(s):

My Question(s):

Check out the See-Through Life DVD Curriculum

Topics in this series include:

- Lesson 1: The Rewards of Being Open
- Lesson 2: The Power of Honesty and Courage
- Lesson 3: The Impact of the Right People
- Lesson 4: For Girls Only/For Guys Only

Learn more and get started at **simplyyouthministry.com**

SEE
—THROUGH—
LIFE